TABLE OF CONTENTS

BEFORE YOU START

> Fixing our eyes on Jesus, the pioneer and perfecter of faith. For the joy set before him he endured the cross, scorning its shame, and sat down at the right hand of the throne of God. Consider him who endured such opposition from sinners, so that you will not grow weary and lose heart.
> – Hebrews 12:2-3

We live in a world ripped apart by Satan's global scheme to destroy the lives of both Muslims and Christians. He will stop at nothing to deceive us, manipulate us, and paralyze us with fear – anything to keep our eyes off Jesus, his purposes, his love, and his provision of hope.

As we are daily battered by the bad news of global calamity, war, and death, hope can seem distant, utopian, and unrealistic. It is easy to raise defensive barriers which unintentionally shut off the joy of living in Christ and stop the flow of his love pouring out towards people who need the good news he has given us. We shrink our reality to the myopic vision of our present, temporal, and personal need. The purpose of this study is to unshackle hearts and attach them again to hope: hope for Muslims to be changed by the unmistakable work of Christ in their lives. And hope for us as well: hope that releases us to be alive with uncontainable joy for today, for the future, for expending ourselves in counter-cultural defiance of Satan's agenda of destruction; and joy as we erect communities declaring that all the wealth and power of heaven is available today – not someday but today – through submission to Christ rather than Islam.

I pray that the Holy Spirit will liberate your heart as you explore his heart for Muslims, research truth in his Word, and refine your purpose in his plan to rescue humanity from Satan – his plan to embrace Muslims with the love of Christ.

Keith E. Swartley kswartley@encounteringislam.org

GETTING READY

A few things should be kept in mind to derive the most benefit from this study:

1. **The Holy Spirit will teach and lead you in the truth.**
   John 14:26, 16:13a; 1 Corinthians 2:10-13

Each time you engage with the Bible, ask the Spirit of truth what you need to see.

2. **The Bible is living, powerful, and transforming.**
   Jeremiah 23:29; 2 Timothy 3:16-17; Hebrews 4:12

3. **Meditation will advance you beyond interpreting the Bible through your biases and filter of need.**
   Ephesians 1:18a; 1 Timothy 4:15

4. **Your community plays a role.**
   1 Thessalonians 5:11

5. **This study includes five basic elements:**

   a. **Prep** – Evaluate your starting point with verses, reflection questions, and personal experience.

   b. **Read** – Gain insight into what God is doing and how you can join.

   c. **Discuss** – Learn with each other through engaging with verses, questions, and your own thoughts.

   d. **Meditate** – Bring these verses and concepts into your life and reflect on them deeply.

   e. **Intercede** – Engage with God by actively interceding on behalf of Muslim peoples.

LESSON 1
WHAT IS GOD'S PLAN FOR MUSLIMS?

"Of course, the overwhelming majority of Muslims are not terrorists or sympathetic to terrorists. Equating all Muslims with terrorism is stupid and wrong. But acknowledging that there is a link between Islam and terror is appropriate and necessary."
– *Ayaan Hirsi Ali (born 1969)*

PREP

What is God's plan? We might be able to sleep better at night if we had a clearer picture of his purposes in Afghanistan, Iraq, Nigeria, Syria, and Yemen, though we are not saying God planned terrorism. "And we know that in all things God works for the good of those who love him, who have been called according to his purpose" (Romans 8:28). But this seems too simple, too trite, even a dismissal of the global calamity we see each day on the news. God cannot be unaware of how it came about that there are 2 billion Muslims worldwide.¹ What does he have in mind? Hebrews 6 maintains that our hope, encouragement, and security are found in the very clear, unchanging nature of God's purpose. But if his plan for us is so clear, who will tell us about it and when? We live in fear-producing and unsettling times. So, if God desires that his people find hope, encouragement, and security in his plan, we need to know what it is.

1. **What do you fear?**

   a. List the most important sources of insecurity for you and your friends today.

   b. What are your fears as far as Muslims are concerned?

   c. What do you think God is doing in the Muslim world?

2. **Read Hebrews 6:13-19.**

   a. To whom did God reveal his purpose?

   b. Why did God both promise and take an oath?

   c. What does "an anchor for the soul" mean to you?

READ

MUSLIM BELIEFS

Islam* simply means submission to God, and a **Muslim** is one who submits his will to God by practicing Islam. Islam was given to **Muhammad**, who is revered by Muslims as God's last and greatest prophet. Muhammad was born AD 570 in **Mecca**, a city in present-day Saudi Arabia. His father died before he was born, his mother died when he was only six, and his grandfather died when he was eight. After this, Muhammad was brought up by his poor yet highly respected uncle, Abu Talib.

Idol worship abounded among the nomadic Arab tribes. Mecca was a major center of idolatry in the region. Muslim historians record that even as a boy Muhammad detested idol worship and lived a morally pure life. Think about Muhammad's childhood experiences and how these may have shaped him. Muhammad became known as "Al-Amin," the trustworthy one, for his honesty and his ability to negotiate disputes amid a feudal society. He was employed by **Khadija**, a wealthy widow fifteen years his senior, to manage her caravan trade. When Muhammad was twenty-five years old, Khadija proposed marriage. Muhammad and Khadija were married for twenty-five years and had six children, although all except the youngest daughter (**Fatima**) died very young.

After such a difficult childhood, the now married and wealthy Muhammad was often depressed and wandered alone in the desert. During one of these retreats, in a cave on the slopes of Mount Hira, several kilometers from Mecca, Muhammad began to receive revelation and instruction from a supernatural being. At first, Muhammad was afraid of these revelations and doubted that he was a prophet. Others encouraged him, however, and these revelations eventually became the **Qur'an**. In addition to the Qur'an, Muslims rely on traditions called **hadiths** about the life, teachings, and practices of Muhammad. These traditions influence the daily life of most Muslims in varying degrees.

After his supernatural experiences began in AD 610, Muhammad began to preach in Mecca against the idolatry of the Arab tribes and the mistreatment of widows, orphans, and the poor by those who were rich, including his own tribe. For his outspokenness, he and many of his early followers were disowned, persecuted, and exiled. Several were even martyred. Eventually, Muhammad fled with his followers to become the political and religious leader of **Medina**, a city 270 miles north of Mecca. Here Islamic prayers were begun, the first **mosque** was erected, and an annual pilgrimage to Mecca was instituted. Muhammad saw this flight from suffering as God's deliverance and the beginning of success in creating a perfect Muslim society.

Muhammad proclaimed that the Qur'an was the final and superior revelation from the One Supreme God. He banned the worship of idols and taught that a Muslim's life must be wholly committed to God, with ritual washing before the five daily times of prayer facing Mecca. Friday became the appointed day for corporate worship at the mosque. Muhammad died in AD 632 in Medina, Arabia, several years after returning to conquer Mecca.

Muslims believe in God. The Arabic word for God is Allah. Allah is described as unique, all powerful, gracious, and merciful by Muslims. The Islamic faith is lived out through five **pillars** that must be followed if one hopes for salvation.

THE FIVE PILLARS ARE:

1. **Reciting the Muslim creed** (*Shahada*) – **"There is no God but God, and Muhammad is his prophet."**

2. **Prayer** (*salat*) – **At five set times each day.**

3. **Almsgiving** (*zakat*) – **Both obligatory and voluntary giving to the poor.**

4. **Fasting** (*saum*) – **Especially during the "holy" month of Ramadan.**

5. **Pilgrimage** (*hajj*) – **At least once in a lifetime to Mecca.**

Although a Muslim may observe all of these practices, Islam still does not guarantee salvation. There is no atonement for sin in Islam, and Muslims generally believe that they should perform religious acts so that their good works will outweigh their bad deeds on the Day of Judgment. Even then, Muslims believe that God's judgment is based on his sovereign will. Muslims lack assurance of forgiveness.

While Muhammad is Islam's last and greatest prophet, the Qur'an also speaks often of Jesus, who is known as *Isa*.

*

The Qur'an refers to Jesus as *Kalimat Allah*, which means "the Word of God." Muslims believe that Jesus was born by a miracle of God through the virgin Mary. However, Muslims do not believe in Christ's death on the cross, his resurrection, or his deity. Although Jesus is the second highest prophet in Islam, the Isa of the Qur'an is only one prophet among God's many prophets. While Muslims respect Christians and Jews as believers in God, Muslims were mistreated by western *Crusaders* and later western imperialists who called themselves Christians. Today many Muslims do not understand how Christians who claim to follow Christ can permit their countries to export pornography or continue to economically dominate the poor.

Belief in angels and evil spirits plays a prominent role in the lives of most Muslims. Islam generally teaches that "all good and evil comes from God," so fatalism is at the heart of the Muslim faith and experience. Honor and shame are also important values within the Muslim community.

MAJOR MUSLIM PEOPLE GROUPS AND AFFINITY BLOCS

A **people group** is an ethno-linguistic group with a common self-identity shared by the various members. For strategic purposes, it is the largest group within which the gospel can spread without encountering barriers of understanding or acceptance.[2] There are about 2,400 Muslim people groups with a total population of two billion Muslims.[3] All people groups are then subsets in a particular region with others of similar cultural roots. And Muslims are grouped into seven **affinity blocs** based on language, culture, religion, politics. In nearly every bloc exist widely dissimilar and unrelated linguistic minorities, but often there is one particular culture that is dominant.

AFFINITY BLOCS

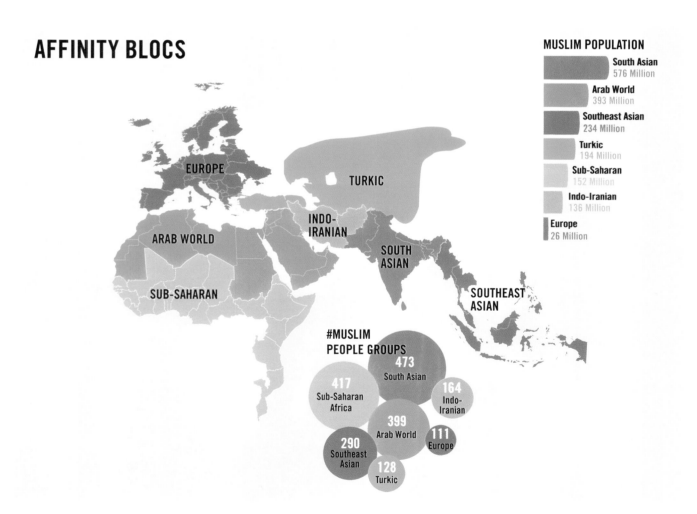

MUSLIM POPULATION

South Asian 576 Million
Arab World 393 Million
Southeast Asian 234 Million
Turkic 194 Million
Sub-Saharan 152 Million
Indo-Iranian 136 Million
Europe 26 Million

EUROPE
TURKIC
INDO-IRANIAN
ARAB WORLD
SOUTH ASIAN
SUB-SAHARAN
SOUTHEAST ASIAN

#MUSLIM PEOPLE GROUPS

473 South Asian
417 Sub-Saharan Africa
164 Indo-Iranian
399 Arab World
111 Europe
290 Southeast Asian
128 Turkic

Ninety-four percent of all Muslims live in these sixty-eight countries

Country	Muslim Population (by millions)	Percentage Muslim
Indonesia	229	88%
Pakistan	200	97%
India	195	14%
Bangladesh	154	90%
Nigeria	99	50%
Egypt	88	92%
Iran	83	99%
Turkey	80	99%
Algeria	41	99%
Sudan	40	97%
Iraq	38	96%
Morocco	38	99%
Ethiopia	36	34%
Afghanistan	35	100%
Saudi Arabia	32	97%
China	28	2%
Yemen	28	99%
Uzbekistan	27	96%
Niger	21	98%
Russia	20	14%
Tanzania	19	35%
Mali	18	95%
Syria	17	93%
Malaysia	16	61%
Senegal	15	96%
Kazakhstan	13	70%
Democratic Republic of Congo	13	10%
Burkina Faso	12	62%
Côte d'Ivoire	11	43%
Tunisia	11	100%
Somalia	11	100%
Guinea	11	89%
Jordan	10	97%
Azerbaijan	10	97%

Country	Muslim Population (by millions)	Percentage Muslim
Chad	9.2	58%
Philippines	7.9	8%
Cameroon	7.7	30%
Tajikistan	7.6	97%
Libya	6.5	97%
Sierra Leone	6.1	79%
France	5.7	9%
Kenya	5.5	11%
Uganda	5.4	14%
Ghana	5.1	18%
Turkmenistan	4.8	93%
Germany	4.8	6%
Kyrgyzstan	4.7	80%
United Arab Emirates	4.6	76%
Palestine	4.3	98%
United Kingdom	4.1	6%
Malawi	4	20%
Mauritania	3.8	100%
Mozambique	3.8	18%
Lebanon	3.5	58%
United States	3.5	1%
Benin	3.1	28%
Cambodia	3.1	2%
Thailand	3	4%
Italy	3	5%
Eritrea	2.6	44%
Madegascar	2.6	10%
South Sudan	2.5	20%
Oman	2.4	86%
Myanmar	2.4	4%
Kuwait	2.2	75%
Sri Lanka	2.1	10%
Gambia	2	96%

SOURCE

https://worldpopulationreview.com/country-rankings/muslim-population-by-country/

INTERCEDE

OVERVIEW OF MUSLIMS TODAY

People often think that most Muslims are Arab and live in the "Middle East," but the Muslim world is much more diverse. The two billion Muslims[4] alive today live in every part of the globe and make up 25 percent of the world's population.[5] Arabic is the primary language of around 350 million people across North Africa, the Arabian Peninsula, and Southwest Asia, making it the fifth most widely spoken language in the world.[6] Yet Arabic is the native language of only 20 percent of Muslims.

The four countries with the largest Muslim populations are Indonesia (228 million), Pakistan (200 million), India (186 million), and Bangladesh (146 million).[7] Iran, Turkey, Egypt, and Nigeria are each home to between 79 and 86 million Muslims.[8] Altogether, forty-nine countries have a Muslim majority.[9] Another twenty-four countries have more than two million Muslims. China has 29 million and Russia has 17 million.[10]

While the most Muslims live in Asia (986 million), the Arab World (317 million), and Sub-Saharan Africa (248 million), a growing number make their homes in countries like France, Germany, the United Kingdom, and the United States.[11] Europe has 43 million[12] Muslims and the United States has around 3.5 million.[13] The world's Muslim population is growing 1.9 percent per year, largely through high birthrates.[14] The majority of Muslims (87-90 percent) are *Sunni* Muslims and 10-13 percent are *Shi`a*.[15] Many Muslims suffer from lack of food and clean water, illiteracy and poor education, poor health care, poverty, natural disasters, and a lack of basic human rights.

- Pray that God would alleviate the physical suffering of Muslims.

- Pray that God would protect and strengthen Muslim background believers as they demonstrate their faith in Christ by their behavior and their words of hope.

- Pray that the Holy Spirit will move hearts of Christians, so that they will reach out to Muslims with the same unconditional acceptance with which Christ loves us.

DISCUSS

1. **Turn to the promise referred to in Hebrews 6, which is first recorded in Genesis 12:1-3.**

    a. How did God's covenant with Abraham differ from the kind of contract we agree to when we buy property?

    b. Why did God include a promise with his instruction to Abraham?

    c. Why has God blessed Abraham?

    d. Who are the families to whom Abraham's descendants are to be a blessing?

2. **Read God's oath in Genesis 22:15-18.**

    a. What is foreshadowed by this drama surrounding God's oath?

    b. How will "all nations" be blessed by Abraham's obedience?

c. What do Genesis 12 and 22 tell us about God's unchanging purpose?

3. Has God predicted the fulfillment of his promise and oath? Read Revelation 5:9-10 and 7:9-10.

    a. Name two aspects of the fulfillment of God's promise.

    b. What evidence can you cite that God will be faithful in fulfilling his covenant promise?

    c. How do Muslim tribes, nations, and peoples figure into his promise?

    d. Who was present at the early church's experience recorded in Acts 2:1-12?

4. Answer in light of what you have seen in Genesis and Revelation.

    a. What new insights do you have about the Great Commission in Matthew 28:18-20?

    b. What is the significance of defining the extent of the blessing as "all nations" (*goyim* in Genesis 22:18 and *ethne* in Matthew 28:19 and Revelation 5:9)? Note: *goyim* is the Hebrew word for the non-Jewish peoples; *ethne*, as used in the Greek translation of the Old Testament and in the New Testament, indicates peoples (people groups), not geographic territories.

    c. What further clarification of God's unchanging purpose is given in Galatians 3:8, 14?

5. The unchanging purpose of God and his promise of standing side by side with believers from Muslim backgrounds from each and every ethnicity ought to establish our hope and free us to pursue relationships with Muslims. Remember that, just as we do, Muslims connect the roots of their faith to Abraham, but note that they trace God's blessing through Ishmael rather than Isaac.

    a. Read Genesis 17:20, 21:13-18, and 25:12-16. What is God's plan for Ishmael and his descendants? Write down the names of the sons of Ishmael (needed for question 6b).

    b. Is God's blessing, provision, and purpose for Ishmael's sons different from those he planned for Abraham and Isaac (Genesis 17:19, 21) and their descendants?

    c. If Ishmael and his sons are still to be blessed by God, what implication does that have for us today?

    d. What purpose could God have in his plan for blessing Muslims?

6. **Look at another prophecy in Isaiah 60:1-22.**

    a. What future events are pictured in this passage?

    b. Whose sons are Kedar and Nebaioth, and what are they doing? (See question 5a.)

7. **We tend to track the spread of the gospel through Paul as starting in Antioch (Acts 13) and moving westward toward Rome. Now look at Acts 9:19-30, Galatians 1:16-24, and 2 Corinthians 11:32-33.**

    a. What do these verses add?

    b. Why do you think we focus on Paul's missionary journeys west?

    c. What does the governor's attempt to arrest Paul in Damascus tell you about the nature of his early missionary activity in Arabia and Syria?

    d. What was Paul's immediate response to the mission God gave him to preach God's Son to the Gentiles? Which Gentiles did he go to first?

MEDITATE

1. **Reflect on your usual sources of hope, encouragement, and security. What are they?**

2. **Memorize Hebrews 6:17-18: "Because God wanted to make the unchanging nature of his purpose very clear to the heirs of what was promised, he confirmed it with an oath. God did this so that, by two unchangeable things in which it is impossible for God to lie, we who have fled to take hold of the hope set before us may be greatly encouraged."**

3. **Write down some of your thoughts about what God is saying to you through this passage this week.**

4. **How might you apply these insights to your daily life?**

5. **How might these truths affect your view of current events in the Muslim world?**

"Hope is called the anchor of the soul (Hebrews 6:19), because it gives stability to the Christian life. But hope is not simply a 'wish' (I wish that such-and-such would take place); rather, it is that which latches on to the certainty of the promises of the future that God has made."
– RC Sproul (1939-2017)

BIBLICAL VALUES MUSLIMS AND CHRISTIANS SHARE

"I like your Christ; I do not like your Christians. Your Christians are so unlike your Christ."
– *Mohandas Gandhi (1869-1948)*

PREP

1. **Many times we describe Christians as being what they ought to be like. Most of the world has a startlingly different perspective. Their experiences and observations of people who call themselves "Christians" have led them to the conclusion that these people do not behave like Christ. Those who are Christians in name only, cultural "Christians," define Christianity for most of the world.**

    a. Characterize this external perception of Christians. Describe its distinguishing attributes.

    b. Specifically, how would a Muslim describe Christians?

    c. What do you think about how Christians are perceived?

    d. Is this a fair assessment of Christianity?

    e. What has shaped this perception of Christianity?

READ

UNREACHED AND UNENGAGED

An unreached people group (UPG) is an identifiable group of people distinguished by a distinct culture, language, or social class who lack a community (at least 2 percent, as measured by https://www.peoplegroups.org) of Evangelical Christians able to evangelize the rest of the people group without outside help.[16] As many as 2,200 Muslim people groups fall into this category and are called "Muslim unreached people groups" (MUPG).[17]

Unreached people groups (UPG) lack a reproducing, self-sustaining, church planting movement within their own culture.[18] Half of MUPGs have no confirmed church planting underway so we call them "Muslim *unengaged* unreached people groups" (MUUPG).[19]

There are many MUPGs that are engaged (about 1,100 peoples).[20] This means that they have at least one church planting team that is active. In many of these people groups, the first teams struggle just to share the good news of Jesus Christ with the people they know. Many more helpers are needed on these teams so that additional churches can be established. Perhaps God is calling you to join in engaging the engaged but under-served. While one out of every three non-Christians is a Muslim, approximately 10 percent of the world's mission force is focused on Muslims.[21] However, despite the lack of witness among Muslims, more Muslims have become followers of Christ in the last thirty years than in the previous 1250 years. Evangelical Christianity is growing by evangelism at a greater rate than Islam!

By 2025, Vision 5:9 partners seek effective churches among all Muslim people groups. To reach our goal, we must establish church planting teams among Muslim people groups who have none.

The following infographic describes the process of reaching UPGs as a fruit of abiding in Christ:

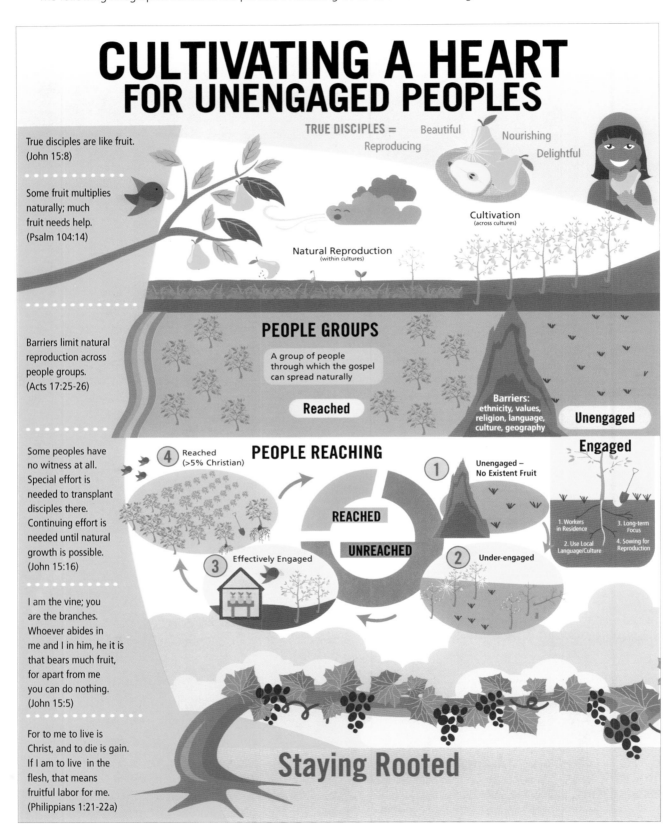

DISCUSS

1. One way the gospel is expressed in the Bible is in terms of Christ's being punished for our sins in our stead, thereby making us right with God. Therefore, part of our concept of justice is in terms of right and wrong (Romans 2:13). We do not like it when we feel wronged or are perceived or treated unfairly. The gospel also addresses the joint issues of honor and shame, another part of justice.

   a. What is the difference between experiencing our personal sin and experiencing shame?

   b. How is this concept of shame and restoration of honor represented in:

   The parable of the Lost Son in Luke 15:11-31?

   The incident of Christ's conversation with the woman at the well in John 4:1-42?

   The account of Adam and Eve in Genesis 2-3?

   c. Often the concept of God "shining his face" on us is considered as blessing and favor, such as in Numbers 6:24-26. Consider the emotions one feels when God's face "shine[s] on" us in Ephesians 5:13b or is turned away. How does Eph. 5:13b add to our biblical view of a good name, status, blessing, or defilement? What does it mean in this context for God's face to be on you?

   d. How has this understanding of shame expanded your understanding of redemption?

2. Muslim communities resonate with a strong awareness of family honor. Dishonor must be hidden or avenged. Muslims' view of Christianity is colored by their sense that, for example, Christ's suffering and dying on the cross are shameful. They believe that God could not possibly allow his prophet to suffer such disgrace or injustice.

   a. Restate the gospel (the redemption achieved by Christ's sacrifice, offered in love) in terms of shame and honor, instead of sin and forgiveness.

   b. How could you use Hebrews 12:2, or passages like it, to help a Muslim rethink his impression of the cross as shameful?

3. Consider other values of the Muslim community and how these reflect biblical values. For each, give a biblical example which shows the same values.

   a. Hospitality and generosity

   b. Extended family and community

    c. Tradition (as a positive value)

    d. Indirect communication

4. **In addition to honor, Muslims also respect supernatural beings and forces (e.g., angels, dreams, miracles). They live under "fate" and fear events beyond their control. Muslims conclude that Christians discount the supernatural – which, in fact, many of us do.**

    a. How would you use Colossians 1:15-17 to explain that Christians believe the world is controlled by the supernatural?

    b. Matthew 21:18-22?

    c. Matthew 8:14-17?

5. **The gospel saves us from the consequences of our sin and rebellion, but other results are achieved by the gospel besides removal of our guilt and shame and alleviation of our fear.**

    a. What results are described by Romans 8:15-17 and Ephesians 1:4-6?

    b. What benefits are specified in Romans 6:22?

MEDITATE

1. **What does it mean that we are victorious in Christ (1 Corinthians 15:57)?**

2. **Memorize Hebrews 12:2: "Fixing our eyes on Jesus, the pioneer and perfecter of faith. For the joy set before him he endured the cross, scorning its shame, and sat down at the right hand of the throne of God."**

INTERCEDE

WHERE IS THE MIDDLE EAST?

The *Far East*, the *Sub-Continent*, the *Near East*, and the *Middle East*. Each of these terms has been used to specify parts of Asia and even Africa. But such designations do not have commonly accepted meanings and often carry negative connotations for the peoples who live in the areas described. Territories labeled "the Far East" and "the Sub-Continent" are better described as East Asia and South Asia. However, "the Near East," and especially "the Middle East," do not have clear, alternative names.

At times "the Near East" is said to include Central Asia (the "-stan" countries) and Iran (*Persia*). Sometimes Iran, Pakistan, and Afghanistan are included as part of "the Middle East," although they are linguistically, historically, and culturally distinct from Arabic-speaking countries. Because of North Africa's linguistic ties to Arabia and Turkey's historic connections (through the *Ottoman* Empire), they also are mislabeled part of "the Middle East," though Turks (and Iranians) typically do not care to be referred to as Middle Easterners.

Modern Turkey does have a distinct geographic name: ***Anatolia*** or ***Asia Minor***. So do Saudi Arabia, Yemen, and the other Arab Gulf states: the Arabian Peninsula. Terms like Anatolia, Arabian Peninsula, Central Asia, North Africa, and Persia are accurate for these geographic regions and acceptable to their inhabitants. Updating our nomenclature is appropriate. (For example, we no longer call Southeast Asia "Indochina"). Though referring to Iraq (ancient Mesopotamia), Israel, Jordan, Lebanon, Palestine, and Syria as "***Southwest Asia***" may seem awkward, this designation is more accurate than "the Middle East."

- Pray that geographic, linguistic, and cultural distinctions would not hinder the spread of good news in the Muslim world and that God would reveal himself to every people group in this region.

- Pray that faith in Jesus would bring new hope, identity, and unity to the peoples of North Africa, Southwest Asia, and the Arabian Peninsula.

"When neither their property nor their honor is touched, the majority of men live content."
– Niccolo Machiavelli (1469-1527), The Prince

LESSON 3
RESPONDING TO INJUSTICE?

"When the missionaries came to Africa, they had the Bible and we had the land. They said, 'Let us pray.' We closed our eyes. When we opened them, we had the Bible and they had the land."
– Desmond Tutu (born 1931)

PREP

1. Muslims around the world feel oppressed. Many have been humiliated by foreign domination. Most Muslims are also poor and suffer disaster and disease without opportunities for the political freedom, education, housing, food, clean water, and medical care we consider basic. God has consistently demanded from his people a high standard of justice and mercy toward the oppressed. Look at his heart for the oppressed embodied in his fundamental law in Deuteronomy 24:17-22.

   a. What classes of people were to be protected by God's people?

   b. What special privileges were they to be given?

   c. What final reminder of the need to be compassionate is given in verse 22?

READ

1. Read Matthew 23 and James 2.

2. The graphic on the following page describes unengaged peoples as fields waiting to be planted.

WHERE THERE IS NO WITNESS... PLANT A FIELD!

Reaching the Unengaged

Unengaged people groups are like empty fields. To see a spiritual orchard develop and bear fruit that multiplies we must:

▶ Survey the empty fields.

152 million Muslims have no resident witness for Christ.

100%
44% OTHER
56% MUSLIM UNENGAGED UNREACHED
2022 Data

Of The 20 Largest Unengaged Unreached People Groups, 16 Of Them Are Majority Muslim.[1]

He turns a desert into pools of water, a parched land into springs of water... they sow fields and plant vineyards and get a fruitful yield.
Psalm 107:35, 37

▶ Understand unengaged soils.

NOMADIC PEOPLES
Challenges: Access, lifestyle
Examples: • Awadhi Gujjar of India (407,000)
• Zaghawa of Sudan (152,000)

IMMIGRANT PEOPLES
Challenges: Mastering 2+ cultures
Examples: • Wolof of Italy (80,000)
• Urdu of Bahrain (64,000)

ISOLATED PEOPLES
Challenges: Access, communication
Examples: • Deaf Turks of Turkey (278,000)
• Buol of Indonesia (96,000)

RESTRICTED PEOPLES
Challenges: Restrictions, unrest
Examples: • Socotran of Yemen (115,000)
• Khunsari of Iran (23,500)

Millions of unengaged Muslims live in every region.

Europe 32%
Central Asia 37%
Middle East/N. Africa 63%
Sahel 63%
Sub-Saharan Africa 28%
South Asia 27%
Southeast Asia 29%

% Groups Unengaged

Population within Unengaged Groups
> 30,000,001 (19)
20,000,001 to 30,000,000 (0)
10,000,001 to 20,000,000 (56)
5,000,001 to 10,000,000 (6)
< 5,000,000 (53)

▶ Transplant hardy believers.

3%
Only 3% of missionaries work among Muslim unreached peoples.

What helps cross-cultural workers last?[3]
● Physical and Psychological Health
● Local Church Ministry Experience
● Bible or Missions Training

250+
It isn't easy, but 250+ Muslim people groups have been engaged since 2008. Who makes it happen? The Holy Spirit in healthy, hardy, adaptable servants supported by mobilizing agencies.[2]

Who is well suited for transplanting?

Culturally Similar Peoples
Similar appearance or lifestyle

Proximate Peoples
Close in geography and perspective

Diaspora Peoples
Returnees who found Christ

Foreigners
Gifted, prepared and incarnational

▶ Plant in season!

Some opportunities are sought; others arise unexpectedly

WINTER — Media/Internet
SPRING — Social/Health Services
FALL — Relief/Compassion Work
SUMMER — Transformational Business

ARE YOU READY TO PLANT A FIELD?

LEARN & PRAY
http://peoplegroups.org/

SHARE A VIDEO
https://vimeo.com/77505312

DISCOVER PEOPLES NEAR YOU
https://www.peoplegroups.info/site/MetroAreaList

CHALLENGE YOUR CHURCH OR AGENCY
http://issacharinitiative.org/count/organizations/

Engage Today!

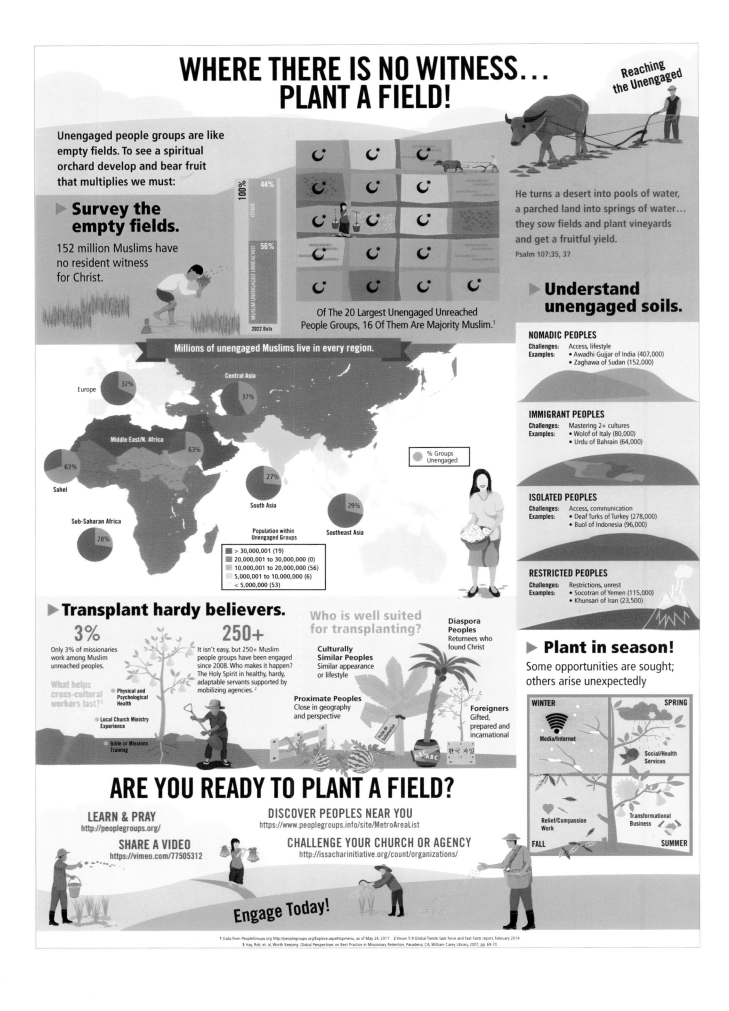

1 Data from PeopleGroups.org http://peoplegroups.org/Explore.aspx#topmenu, as of May 24, 2017. 2 Vision 5:9 Global Trends task force and Fast Facts report, February 2014.
3 Hay, Rob, et. al, Worth Keeping: Global Perspectives on Best Practice in Missionary Retention, Pasadena, CA, William Carey Library, 2007, pp. 69-70.

DISCUSS

1. **Refer back to Matthew 23.**

    a. Christ was very critical of the religious. If he entered your home, what might he point out?

    b. What would he find to criticize about our churches?

    c. By which of our values and priorities might we be embarrassed?

    d. Of the values of "justice, mercy, and faithfulness," which is most important to you? Explain why.

2. **Refer back to James 2:1-26. Smug elitism, racial arrogance, disdain for the poor, favoritism of the wealthy, lack of mercy, moral or personal judgmental attitude, and hypocrisy are the ugliest of behaviors. Interestingly, we find it much easier to identify these in others than in ourselves.**

    a. What impression do Christians who behave this way, or stand silently by as others exhibit these behaviors, make upon you?

    b. What verdict does James pass on these believers?

3. **In Luke 4, Christ visits his hometown and his teaching in the synagogue turns those assembled from admiration to rage, so much so that they try to kill him. On the basis of their pride in their heritage and knowledge, they believed they deserved God's favor. Christ conveyed a disturbingly different point. Read Luke 4:14-30.**

    a. For whom is God concerned?

    b. Who will receive (needs) God's deliverance (favor)?

    c. What is "the year of the Lord's favor"? See Leviticus 25:10

    d. How should you declare God's deliverance to the poor, the imprisoned, the blind, and the oppressed?

    e. By whom are these groups of people represented today in our world and your community?

MEDITATE

1. **Meditate on the quote from Isaiah in Luke 4:18-19.**

2. **Memorize Micah 6:8: "He has shown you, O mortal, what is good. And what does the Lord require of you? To act justly and to love mercy and to walk humbly with your God."**

INTERCEDE

OVERVIEW OF ARABIC-SPEAKING PEOPLES

Many people associate Muslims with the Arab world. Although the majority of Muslims worldwide are not Arab, Islam is rooted in the Arab culture and language of its founder, Muhammad. Islam's holiest cities, Mecca and Medina, to which millions of Muslims make pilgrimage each year, are in the Arabian Peninsula.

North Africa, the Arabian Peninsula, and Southwest Asia contain twenty Arabic-speaking countries, with 420 million people.[22] The countries which compose the Arab world are home to diverse people groups – including Arabs, Berbers, and Bedouin groups, the Druze, the Tuareg peoples, and the Egyptians.

Most Egyptians were Christians until a few hundred years after the beginning of Islam. Today 92 percent are Muslims.[23] Most of Egypt's 106 million people[24] live in the fertile Nile Valley which has some of the highest population densities in the world. The majority of Egyptians are still *fellahin*, or farmers. While some Egyptians still wear traditional dress of ankle-length tunics, many men in the cities have adopted blue jeans and athletic shoes.

Other significant Arab concentrations are found in Australia, Canada, the United Kingdom, the United States and Venezuela. There are 86 million people in 287 unengaged unreached people in the Arab World.[25]

PRAYER POINTS:

- During the first centuries AD there was a strong church in North Africa. Church divisions, heresy, and its shallow roots eventually toppled it, and Islam took over. Pray that Arabic-speaking Christians would be united, steadfast, and eager to witness of Christ.

- Ask the Lord to send more Christian workers, to grant them perseverance to stay in difficult environments and wisdom to sow biblical truth effectively.

- Pray that Muslims would be moved through dreams and miracles to read the Bible and seek Christ.

For more information: https://www.peoplegroups.org

"True compassion is more than flinging a coin to a beggar; it is not haphazard and superficial. It comes to see that an edifice that produces beggars needs restructuring."
– *Martin Luther King, Jr. (1929–1968)*

LESSON 4
GOOD WORKS AND GODLY LIVING

"Good works do not make a good man, but a good man does good works."
– Martin Luther (1483–1546)

PREP

1. Islam emphasizes its five universal religious practices. We may observe them performing these meritorious works: declaring their belief in God, praying, fasting, giving to the poor, and going on pilgrimage. Even though the emphasis in Christianity is on Christ and his work on our behalf, Christians are also "to practice … 'acts of righteousness,'" express their belief, pray, fast, and support the poor. Read Matthew 6:1-18.

   a. Do you regularly give to the poor, pray, and fast? Describe how you practice these spiritual disciplines.

   b. Describe the right spirit one should have when giving to the poor, praying, and fasting.

   c. What behaviors and attitudes are to be avoided when one is engaged in performing these Christian practices, and why?

READ
MEASURING ENGAGEMENT

Now we understand about people groups, whether they are unreached or unengaged, and the need to engage them with church planting efforts and to prioritize Muslim unengaged unreached people groups (MUUPGs). The Vision 5:9 Global Trends task force has developed this description scale to outline the move from unengaged to engaged, reached, and thriving:

1. **Unengaged**

   * As far as we are aware there is no effort to make disciples among this people with the intention of seeing a church planting movement.

2. **Initial Engagement and Abundant Seed Sowing**

   * A pioneer church planting effort in residence.

   * A commitment to work in the local language and culture.

   * A commitment to long-term ministry.

   * Sowing in a manner consistent with the goal of seeing a church planting movement (CPM) emerge.

3. **Baptized Believers (and ongoing discipleship)**

   * New believers are being discipled and baptized.

4. First Gatherings

- Baptized believers are gathering in fellowships and continue to grow as disciples of Jesus.

- Discipleship reinforces making new disciples and starting new fellowships.

5. Multi-generational Gatherings

- Fellowships of baptized believers are multiplying and starting new fellowships. Expectation of seeing generational growth.

6. Majority of Disciples and Gatherings have Characteristics of Acts 2:36-47 – Disciples Being Sent Out

- The disciples and churches exhibit the nature of the Church in their lives, interaction with one another, and in the communities where they live. Disciples from this movement of churches are being sent out cross-culturally to other people groups as part of the Great Commission labor force.

Read Ephesians 2:4-10.

a. What does this passage say about works?

b. What is one outcome mentioned here that is not the result of works?

c. According to verse 10, works are clearly important. What is their purpose?

DISCUSS

1. **While Christians are instructed to follow practices similar to those Muslims pursue (praying, supporting the poor, and so forth), these works are Christ's work, not our own. While our good behavior does not make us righteous before God, Christians must do good works. Read 1 Peter 2:12.**

    a. Reflect and then record a few thoughts on what you would need to do in order for people to clearly "see your good deeds and glorify God."

    b. Since we cannot "live such good lives" in a moment, how long might this scrutiny take?

    c. What is to be the result, and when might this occur?

2. **Another value Muslims hold dear is community, or *umma*. Islam is thought of as "the best community on earth," and its social integration a reflection of God's oneness, or *tawhid*. Read John 17:20-21.**

    a. What is Christ's prayer for us?

    b. Why does he ask for this? What result is intended?

3. **Envision Christians so closely following Christ that our behavior alone motivates Muslims to follow Christ.**

   a. What steps would be necessary for this to happen?

   b. What can Christians do that would demonstrate their obedience to Christ and their community with each other?

MEDITATE

1. **Revisit the concept of Christians reflecting Christ's love and behavior unambiguously. Do you have any new thoughts?**

2. **Memorize 1 Peter 2:12: "Live such good lives among the pagans that, though they accuse you of doing wrong, they may see your good deeds and glorify God on the day he visits us."**

INTERCEDE

OVERVIEW OF SOUTH ASIAN MUSLIMS

The 1.9 billion Indo-Aryan peoples of South Asia live in the countries of Bangladesh, India, and Pakistan. South Asia is the heart of the Muslim world, home to three of the four largest Muslim populations and a total of over 600 million adherents of Islam, nearly one third of all Muslims.[26] Like the Hindus, Muslims of South Asia are divided by caste. In India, 195 million Muslims are a persecuted minority (14 percent).[27] Major Muslim peoples include the Assamese, Bengali, Bihari, Jat, Kashmiri, Maldivian, Punjabi, Rajasthani, and Sindhi. Large numbers of Urdu speakers also live in Saudi Arabia and other Arabian Gulf states. There are 47 million people in 1,025 unengaged unreached people groups in South Asia.[28]

One significant Muslim people group of this region is the Ansari, estimated to be around 14 million.[29] Historically, the Ansari are weavers. They create the silks and carpets, as well as other handicrafts, for which their lands are famous.

Most of the Ansari live in small towns and villages in the northern states of India where they form close-knit, stable communities. Some work at skilled crafts such as brass and woodworking, while others farm or run small businesses. Like most of India's Muslims, they tend to be poor and are considered low in caste. To deal with the supernatural, they perform rituals of spiritism in order to ward off evil. Traditionally, an Ansari home is led by the eldest male who makes decisions involving his sons and their wives and children.

PRAYER POINTS:

- Pray for God to miraculously relieve the grinding poverty, natural disasters, and epidemic diseases which maim the lives of South Asian Muslims.

- Pray that God would move Christians, who are wealthy by comparison, to use the blessings God has given them to alleviate the social conditions of Muslims in the name of Christ.

- Pray that God would break the satanic oppression which fills Muslims with fear.

For more information: https://www.peoplegroups.org

"The confession of [my] evil works is the first beginning of good works."
– Saint Augustine (354-430)

LESSON 5
HOW WOULD CHRIST RESPOND TO MUSLIMS?

"Compassion costs. It is easy enough to argue, criticize, and condemn, but redemption is costly, and comfort draws from the deep. Brains can argue, but it takes heart to comfort."
– Samuel Chadwick (1820–1869)

PREP

1. How would you describe Jesus? Write down a few of his characteristics.

2. As we examine Christ and how he would (and we should) respond to Muslims, think back to what people often decide about "Christians" (see lesson 2, question 1), and how their perceptions differ from the Christ you just described. Also review your answers in lesson 4, (questions 1a and 3a, b): What would it take for people around you to perceive his characteristics in you?

3. Sadly, Muslims are limited in seeing and being able to describe the same characteristics of Christ you have mentioned. The barriers that thwart them are fortified by their history, cultures, and languages.

    a. Why are we tempted to assert "facts" about Christianity and to allow the conversation to become contentious?

    b. How does Paul answer accusations which questioned his credentials as an apostle in 2 Corinthians 3:1-3?

READ

TIPS FOR SHARING WITH A MUSLIM

1. **Take time to build a real relationship** – which Muslims value highly – to let your friend see Christ in your actions, attitudes, and daily struggles.

2. **Practice hospitality** – also prized. Spend time over tea, coffee or a meal.

3. **Listen.** A good listener focuses on the friend's concerns and needs. Look for bridges between his or her understanding and biblical truths.

4. **Use creative questions to reveal truth** and assist your friend in critical thinking, in recognizing his or her need for a savior.

5. **Keep communication open by discussing issues you have in common,** not those that divide. Agree whenever possible, especially with anything consistent with the Bible.

6. **Share your testimony** of how God transformed your life through the power of the gospel.

7. **Pray regularly for your friend,** that God will reveal his or her needs to you and that the Holy Spirit will intervene supernaturally in this life. Your words are just one part of God's intervention.

8. **Be a good, loving friend.** Your unconditional love will attract him or her to our best friend, Jesus Christ, in whose hands are the results.

9. **Interact only with the same gender.** Genders are usually separated in Islam and piety and purity respected (as they are in Christianity). Women should dress modestly and not enter a gathering of all men. Men, do not enter a home where no men are present.

10. **Be patient,** a fruit of the indwelling Holy Spirit, who will invite in this Muslim woman or man the desire to know more about Jesus.

11. **Sidestep debate or argument.** Let winning your friend be your goal, not winning the argument. Our message is not about religion and its regimen of rituals or a philosophical system; it is about a relationship with God through Christ. Express your gratitude for, and share, what he has done for you.

12. **Avoid insulting the Qur'an, Muhammad, or Islam.** Humiliation is alienating, but our description of Jesus and his work is appealing and will draw our friend closer to faith.

13. **Be sensitive to your Muslim friend's customs:** how she sits or eats; how he enters a house. Our cultural habits may be an affront to their sensibilities.

14. **Be aware of Islamic practice.** We risk offense by placing Bibles on the floor, putting other objects over them, or marking passages in them.

15. **Christians should not denigrate one another.** Refrain from criticizing other Christians, denominations or ministries.

16. **Uphold the simplicity of the gospel** and of believing in it.

17. **Maintain a consistent lifestyle,** one that reflects that the gospel of Christ is power from God for salvation from sin and deliverance from sin's power.

18. **On the issue of salvation,** pray for a genuine work of the Holy Spirit, the one who seeks and secures followers for Jesus. The issue is not a person's decision, but whether you are letting God use you.

Read 1 Corinthians 1:17-25; 2:1-5, 13-14; and 2 Corinthians 12:5-10.

DISCUSS

1. **We agree that our response to each other and to Christ is a heart response, rather than being simply intellectual.**

   a. Why is it important to address people's hearts?

   b. Why should we rely on God's power in our weakness instead of upon our own ability to convince?

2. **Christ's humanity is as significant as his divinity. We hold that Christ's incarnation – his becoming like us, coming as a frail human – is key to his mission. Read 1 Corinthians 9:19-22 and consider how we might follow Paul's example in our witness.**

    a. What does Paul mean by "I have made myself a slave to everyone"?

    b. How did Paul become "like one not having the law" (v. 21)?

3. **Read Matthew 9:35-36 and John 8:10-11; Christ came with good news, with compassion, without condemnation even for those least appreciated by their culture: those without advocates, the sick, women, and children, for example.**

    a. Why did this shock those around him?

    b. How did they want him to behave?

4. **In addition to his willingness to behave contrary to people's expectations in his ministry, Christ identified with our sin. He demonstrated this willing identification at his baptism and in his suffering and death on the cross. Read 1 Peter 2:18-23 and list guidelines for our behavior as we minister to others, even if we suffer, guidelines which emulate Christ.**

5. **Maybe at this point you are wondering, "But when do we defend our faith or ourselves?" or "What about 'being ready to give an answer,' as in 1 Peter 3:15-18?" Read this passage again and note all the instructions there.**

MEDITATE

Gentleness, respect, and not responding in kind when slandered make for a difficult path to follow while giving Christ-centered answers as to why we put our hope in him. These behaviors demonstrate the same attitude which Christ had. Remember that the chief of Christ's character traits that we are to emulate is love.

1. Read 1 John 4:7-12 and reflect on the attractive power of love in response to any and all treatment.

2. Memorize 1 Peter 2:21-23: "To this you were called, because Christ suffered for you, leaving you an example, that you should follow in his steps. He committed no sin, and no deceit was found in his mouth. When they hurled their insults at him, he did not retaliate; when he suffered, he made no threats. Instead, he entrusted himself to him who judges justly."

INTERCEDE

OVERVIEW OF TURKIC MUSLIMS

The Turkic peoples number more than 197 million people[30] and are widely spread across China, Russia, Turkey and Central Asia – mostly in the countries of Afghanistan, Azerbaijan, Iran, Iraq, Kazakhstan, Kyrgyzstan, Tajikistan, Turkmenistan, Turkey, and Uzbekistan. Significant numbers of Turkic peoples have also formed communities in European countries in such as Austria, Cyprus, Belgium, Macedonia, Moldova, Netherlands, Switzerland, and Ukraine, including 650,000 in Bulgaria, 200,000 in France, 360,000 in the United Kingdom, and 2.2 million Turks now living in Germany.[31] There are 4.4 million people in eighty unengaged unreached people groups in Turkic Central Asia including Bashkir, Qashqai, Tatars, and Uyghurs.[32]

Because the former USSR once ruled a number of the countries that are home to Turkic peoples, the populace in these regions has seen incredible changes since their nations gained autonomy in the last two decades of the twentieth century. One such country, Azerbaijan, earned independence from Russia in 1990. Azerbaijanis in the nation of Azerbaijan almost nine million.[33] Even more, nearly 20 million, live in Iran.[34] Nearly all Azerbaijanis are Muslim.

Baku, the capital city of Azerbaijan, population over two million,[35] is a developed urban center. Its residents experience significant western influence because of the city's international oil trade. Rural villages, however, tend to retain the traditional Azerbaijani lifestyle and customs. The widening cultural gap has become apparent in Baku, since Azerbaijan's war with neighboring Armenia in the early 1990s sent an influx of rural Azerbaijani refugees from Armenian-occupied areas to the city. Baku also draws many rural students to study at its universities.

Azerbaijani people are proud of their extensive heritage of poetry and music. Some Baku streets are named after famous Azerbaijani poets and feature a number of gigantic statues paying tribute to famous writers. Many Azerbaijanis mix their Islamic practices with an ancient form of fire worship, which emerged because the region's abundant natural gas reserves sometimes cause fires to burn spontaneously from the earth.

PRAYER POINTS:

- Pray for God to enable Chinese Christians traveling the Silk Road "back to Jerusalem" to witness effectively for Christ in Central Asia.

- Pray that God would provide economic and political change and religious freedom in the former Soviet republics.

For more information: https://www.peoplegroups.org

"Reason is always a kind of brute force; those who appeal to the head rather than the heart, however pallid and polite, are necessarily men of violence. We speak of 'touching' a man's heart, but we can do nothing to his head but hit it."
– G. K. Chesterton (1874-1936)

LESSON 6
QUESTIONS MUSLIMS ASK

"What good is it, my brothers, if a man claims to have faith but has no deeds?"
– *James, the brother of Jesus Christ (James 2:14)*

PREP

1. Muslims usually have several common objections to the gospel. They often say that the Bible has been changed by Jews and Christians. If a Muslim friend says this to you, gently respond that you treasure the Bible, and that Christians would never allow it to be changed. Of course, no human can change God's words. What do these passages say about the changing of the Bible?

   a. Matthew 5:18

   b. Matthew 24:35

   c. Revelation 22:18-19

2. Another frequent criticism Muslims pose is that God is one, not three. This speaks of confusion about the Trinity. If asked this question, reassure your friend that we believe that God is one, and then read Deuteronomy 6:4 together. We do believe in the triune nature of God, and though Muslims may continue to object, we do have a biblical basis for this doctrine. Write out how the following passages reinforce the teaching of God's triune nature.

   a. Isaiah 63:8-10

   b. Matthew 3:16-17

   c. Matthew 28:19

   d. 2 Corinthians 13:14

READ
OVERVIEW OF MALAY PEOPLES

More than 398 million Malay live in the Southeast Asian island nations of Brunei, Indonesia, Malaysia, the Philippines, and Singapore.[36] About 6 million Malay people are unengaged and unreached in ninety-eight people groups.[37]

Islam is the state religion in Brunei, whereas Singapore allows relative freedom of religion. In the Philippines, which is 8 percent Muslim,[38] the Catholic Church holds considerable influence. In western Malaysia, Islam is the official religion, but Muslims are a minority in eastern Malaysia. In Indonesia, where 88 percent are Muslim, the government requires all citizens to choose one of five religions: Buddhism, Chinese traditional religion, Protestant or Catholic Christianity, Hinduism, or Islam.

Five million Aceh live in Indonesia's northern Sumatra, and nearly 100 percent are Muslim.[39] They live in rural areas as rice farmers and fishermen and in cities as both manual laborers and government officials. In 1976, some Aceh formed an independence movement, and thousands of lives have been lost in the subsequent guerrilla war against the Indonesian military. The Aceh also face tensions between their traditional Islamic culture, which values high moral standards and community, and the materialistic western lifestyle, which is increasingly familiar in the media. In December 2004, the Aceh were devastated by a tsunami.

PRAYER POINTS:

- Pray for influential Malay leaders to follow Jesus and be examples of faith in their communities.

- Pray that believers in Indonesia would overcome their fear and prejudice to reach out in compassion and genuine friendship to their Muslim neighbors.

- Pray that God would open the hearts of Malay women and that they would be able to influence whole families for Christ (Acts 16:14-15).

For more information: https://www.peoplegroups.org

DISCUSS

1. **While Muslims believe that Jesus Christ is the Messiah, and that he performed miracles and was born of a virgin, they claim that he did not die on the cross and that he was not the Son of God. Review these passages and summarize the biblical teachings.**

   a. Colossians 1:15-22

   b. Colossians 2:6-10

c. Philippians 2:5-11

d. John 1:1-3

e. John 1:29

f. John 10:30

g. 1 Corinthians 5:7

h. Romans 3:21-26

i. 1 Peter 2:21-24

j. 1 Peter 3:18

2. While addressing these and other objections Muslims raise, we need to build a foundation for their understanding of the gospel. Muslims may not ask these exact questions, but we want to enhance their comprehension of the fundamental concepts which lead to Christ. **List here the Bible passage to which you would refer and how you would share each teaching with your Muslim friend.**

a. What is sin?

b. Why is sin a problem which cannot be dealt with or paid for by our own actions?

c. How can God both love and forgive us, and, at the same time, be just and holy?

d. Given that we cannot restore our holiness in God's sight by our own efforts, how does God solve this separation between us?

MEDITATE

1. **Meditate on how God relates to us now that we belong to Jesus Christ? Record your insights.**

2. **Memorize Deuteronomy 6:4: "Hear, O Israel: The Lord our God, the Lord is one."**

OVERVIEW OF PERSIAN-MEDIAN MUSLIMS

Like the Turkic peoples, the Persian-Median peoples are spread across Central Asia. Persian-Median people groups also have substantial populations in Azerbaijan, India, and Syria. Almost a half million Persians now live in the United States.[40]

Persian-Median number more than 182 million people, including the Balochis, Kurds, Pashtuns, Persians, and Tajiks.[41] Approximately 99 percent of the people are Muslim.[42] There are 21 million people in seventy-six unengaged unreached Persian-Median groups.[43]

The Kurds, an estimated 37 million people,[44] live in a region they call Kurdistan, which straddles Armenia, Azerbaijan, Iran, Iraq, Syria, and Turkey. They are the world's largest ethnic group without a nation. Most Kurds live apart from others, in mountainous areas where they can retain their own culture, traditions, and languages. Traditionally nomadic herders, most are now semi-nomadic or settled. The majority practice devout Sunni Islam. As a people, they lack political unity, yet have usually withstood subjugation by other nations without losing their identity. However, in vying for autonomy in the last half of the twentieth century, the Kurds have been used as pawns in war and have suffered genocide multiple times in the hands of the region's governments. As a result, thousands now live in Europe; more than a half million Kurds now live in Germany. Recent openness has resulted in a young but growing church planting movement among the Kurds of northern Iraq.

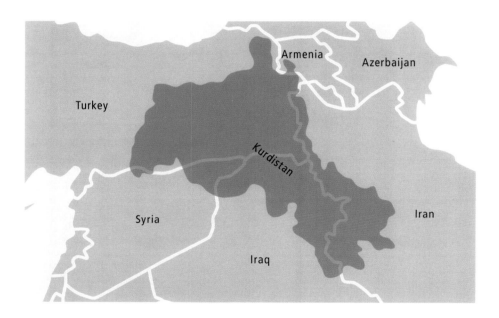

PRAYER POINTS:

- Praise God for, and ask him to protect and mature, fragile communities of believers among the Kurds, Persians, Pushtuns, and Tajiks.

- Pray that God would bring true peace to these war-ravaged peoples and remove the strife between peoples by uniting them in Christ.

- Pray that Christians would be tangible representations of Christ as they live among these peoples.

For more information: https://www.peoplegroups.org

"Lower your voice and strengthen your argument."
– Lebanese Proverb

LESSON 7
SACRIFICE AND SUFFERING

> "Aim at heaven and you will get earth thrown in. Aim at earth and you get neither."
> – C. S. Lewis (1898–1963)

PREP

1. From the beginning of history people have been encouraged to give back to God a portion of what they had received in the form of burnt offerings. Read Genesis 22:1-19 and Hebrews 11:17-19.

   a. What new aspects of offering were introduced on this occasion?

   b. What name of God (given to that place) is revealed during this event (Genesis 22:8, 14)?

   c. What does this event foreshadow (Genesis 22:14, 17-18)?

2. Each year at the end of the Muslim pilgrimage to Mecca, Saudi Arabia, Muslims worldwide celebrate Id al-Adha, the feast of sacrifice commemorating God's miraculous provision of a ram for Ibrahim to sacrifice instead of his son.

   a. What would you ask a Muslim about Id al-Adha to deepen his understanding of the gospel?

   b. What does this event teach us about our relationship with God?

READ
THE FEAST OF SACRIFICE

Every year Muslims around the world celebrate the feast of *Eid al-Adha*, also known as the Feast of Sacrifice or Great Feast (*Eid al-Kabir*), in South Asia as *Bakr Eid*, and in the Turkic world as *Kurban Bayram*. At this time, many Muslims sacrifice a sheep or a goat to commemorate how God redeemed the son of Abraham, as recorded in the Qur'an (Sura 37:99–113).

Judaism teaches about this same event: When Abraham was about to sacrifice his son, "the angel of the Lord called out to him.... Abraham looked up and there in a thicket he saw a ram caught by its horns...and sacrificed it as a burnt offering instead of his son" (Gen. 22:1–19).

Although Jews do not commemorate this specific event with a feast, its meaning is preserved in Passover. Passover is when Jews observe the night that God spared their firstborn from being slain in Egypt. The angel of death "passed over" the houses of those who put the blood of a slaughtered sheep on their doorposts (Ex. 12:1–14).

Since Christians believe in both the Abrahamic sacrifice and the Passover, why don't they celebrate them? Is there a Christian Passover too? The Injil says that human beings are spiritually dead. Sin is the gulf that separates us from

God. Jesus Christ was crucified and died as a righteous sacrifice for the human race. Just as God redeemed the son of Abraham by the sacrifice he provided, the blood of a ram, God redeemed the world through the blood of Jesus Christ. Jesus became the true *Adha*: he was the Lamb of God, sacrificed to set us free from sin, by whom God bridged the gulf that separated us from him.

The events of Adha and Passover were object lessons God used so we could understand true redemption. The Bible says that the blood of calves and sheep will not wash away sins (Heb. 10:14), and that all our good works are like filthy rags compared to God's righteousness (Isa. 64:6). No one can possibly pay the huge debt that is owed to God. The good news is that God sent Jesus Christ to be the perfect sacrificial lamb of God who takes away the sins of the world. Adha and the Passover are remembered in one glorious celebration of the crucifixion and resurrection of Jesus Christ, known in English as *Easter*, and in Arabic as *Eid al-Qiyama*. Jesus Christ is the Adha for people of all nations and races. Through him we can have fellowship with God and experience his love and redemption.

Adapted from Fouad Masri, *Adha in the Injeel*. Used by permission. *fouadmasri.com.*

DISCUSS

1. **The Old Testament feast of Passover commemorates another occasion on which Jehovah Jireh provided for his people through a blood sacrifice. Read Exodus 12:1-14.**

    a. What are the functions of the sacrifice and the blood in the Passover?

    b. Explain God's plan for all humanity as seen in the feast of Passover. See also Luke 22:7-20; 1 Corinthians 5:7, 11:23-26.

2. **Muslims often reject the death of Jesus Christ as being inconsistent with the nature of God. Read John 1:29; Romans 3:25-26, 5:3-11; and 1 John 2:2.**

    a. How would you present Christ's death, in terms of the prescribed Old Testament sacrifices, to a Muslim?

    b. When applied to Christ, why is the Old Testament imagery appropriate?

3. **Muslims teach that by extension of the rule of Islam, people's suffering will be alleviated. In the call to prayer, Muslims are called to success. The Qur'an states that Muslims are "the best of the nations raised up for (the benefit of) men ..." (Qur'an 3:110) Similarly, the Jews (including Christ's disciples), yearned for a Messiah who would lead the overthrow of Rome's dominion and establish a utopian earthly kingdom.**

    a. How did Christ's perspective differ (Matthew 16:21-28, Matthew 24:14 and Acts 1:6-8)?

    b. How will God's kingdom be realized?

4. **We are to participate in all aspects of Christ's life. What do the following passages tell us about that participation?**

   a. 1 Peter 4:12-19; 2 Corinthians 4:11

   b. Romans 8:36; 1 Peter 5:8-9

   c. Hebrews 13:13-16

   d. Colossians 1:24; 2 Timothy 1:8

   e. Romans 8:17

5. **These passages describe the ways Christians behave in the midst of suffering.**

   a. Summarize this conduct.

   b. What would this suffering look like today?

6. **Though we are not instructed to become martyrs or to deliberately provoke strife, the Bible shows us that suffering for Christ is part of the Christian life.**

   a. Account for your own level of suffering, or for the fact that you are not.

   b. What changes in your behavior would make your life more consistent with your profession of faith in the eyes of Muslims (review question 4, especially Hebrews 13:13-16)?

MEDITATE

1. **Reflect on Christ's path of suffering. Reflect on his entire life prior to his death on the cross. Indicate below what you hear God saying.**

2. **Memorize 2 Timothy 2:11-12a: "Here is a trustworthy saying: If we died with him, we will also live with him; if we endure, we will also reign with him.'"**

INTERCEDE

OVERVIEW OF SUB-SAHARAN MUSLIMS INCLUDING THE HORN OF AFRICA

The over one billion people of sub-Saharan Africa[45] – the region just south of Arabic-speaking North Africa – adhere to a wide range of beliefs, including Christianity and animism. Muslim missionary activities over the centuries have extended into sub-Saharan Africa, where currently Islam is the majority religion in twelve countries.[46] About 248 million Muslims live in sub-Saharan Africa.[47] There are 48 million people in 535 unengaged unreached groups in Sub-Saharan Africa[48] and another 18 million in 70 UUPGs in the Horn of Africa.[49]

Some 60 percent of Ethiopians are Christian,[50] but other nations in the Horn of Africa, Djibouti, and Somalia are more than 97 percent Muslim.[51] Christian-Muslim conflict rages along these dividing lines, with atrocities committed on both sides. For example, the non-Arab population of the recently formed (2011) South Sudan is estimated to be 60 percent Christian and 20 percent Muslim, while the Arab-speaking Sudan is 97 percent Muslim.[52]

The Fulani tribes (also called Fula and Fulbe) live all across sub-Saharan Africa, stretching from Senegal to Ethiopia, and form a minority in twenty countries, numbering about 54 million.[53] They are concentrated principally in Nigeria, Mali, Guinea, Cameroon, Senegal, and Niger.[54] The Fulani have a long history as nomadic cattle herdsmen. As one of the first African tribes to follow Islam (seven centuries ago), their nomadic lifestyle helped to spread the religion across much of West Africa. Although they are the largest nomadic-culture people in the world, more than half of the Fulani now live settled lifestyles. Many noted Islamic scholars and teachers are among the educated Fulani, and the urbanized and more affluent tend to be the most orthodox in their beliefs. The majority of Fulani, however, observe a mix of traditional and Islamic beliefs and practices.

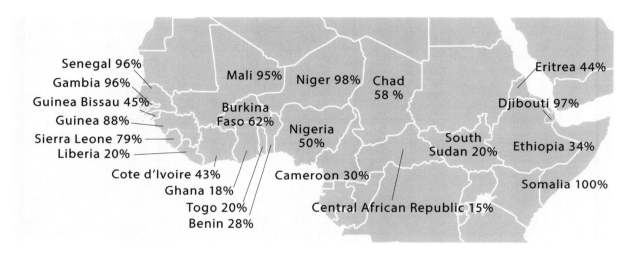

PRAYER POINTS:

- Praise God for his church in Africa and ask him to give Christians compassion for Muslims.

- Pray that God would bring stability to the region and end the scourge of AIDS.

- Pray that Christians would be tangible witnesses of Christ, returning love in the face of evil.

For more information: https://www.peoplegroups.org

"No pain, no palm; no thorns, no throne; no gall, no glory; no cross, no crown."
– *William Penn (1644-1718)*

HOW WILL YOU CONNECT WITH MUSLIMS?

> "We are told to let our light shine, and if it does, we won't need to tell anybody it does. Lighthouses don't fire cannons to call attention to their shining – they just shine."
> – *Dwight L. Moody (1837–1899)*

PREP

1. As we come to the end of our study together, each of us needs to determine how we will connect with Muslims. The sad outcome would be that, after investing the time we have in this study, we did not attempt appropriate actions as a result. Review the responses you have recorded in the previous lessons.

   a. What misconceptions did God correct?

   b. What attitudes did God prompt you to change?

2. Now, having reflected on what God has shown you and remembering that Muslims are looking for Christians who act the way Christ did, imagine some possible steps God may want you to take. Pray that God would reveal his plan to you. Write down what occurs to you, no matter how daring it seems right now.

READ

Hundreds of fruitful church planters from more than forty agencies working across the Muslim world have shared their stories with the Vision5:9 Fruitful Practice Research team. Their activities and priorities have been documented to better understand how God is working through them - and to encourage and train other workers. The following description statements capture many of the lessons learned:

1. **Fruitful Practices Relating to Society**

   • Communicate respect by behaving in culturally appropriate ways.

   • Address tangible needs in their community as an expression of the gospel.

   • Relate to people in ways that respect gender roles in the local culture.

   • Mobilize extensive, intentional, and focused prayer.

   • Pursue language proficiency.

   • Take advantage of pre-field and on-field research to shape their ministry.

   • Build positive relationships with local leaders.

2. Fruitful Practices Relating to Seekers

- Be bold in witness.

- Pray for God's supernatural intervention as a sign that confirms the gospel.

- Pray for the needs of their friends in their presence.

- Share the gospel through existing social networks.

- Begin discipling seekers as part of the process of coming to faith.

- Encourage seekers to share what God is doing in their lives.

3. Fruitful Practices Relating Believers

- Be intentional in their discipling.

- Disciple in locally appropriate and reproducible ways.

- Disciple others in settings that fit the situation.

- Help seekers and believers find appropriate ways to identify themselves to their community as followers of Jesus, without imposing their own preferences.

- Help believers find ways to remain within their social network.

- Encourage believers to develop healthy relationships with other believers.

- Model following Jesus in intentional relationships with believers.

- Encourage believers to follow the Holy Spirit's leading in applying the Bible to their context.

- Encourage believers to share their faith.

- Prepare believers to explain why they believe.

- Model service to others and teach believers to serve others as well.

- Use various approaches in discipling.

- Encourage baptism by other believers with a Muslim background.

- Deal with sin in biblical ways that are culturally appropriate.

4. Fruitful Practices Relating to Leaders

- Acknowledge emerging leaders early in the process of building a community of faith.

- Mentor leaders who in turn mentor others.

- Encourage leadership based on godly character.

- Be intentional about leadership development.

- Use the Bible as the primary source for leadership development.

- Preference developing leaders locally.

5. Fruitful Practices Relating to God

- Practice an intimate walk with God.

- Engage in regular, frequent prayer.

- Persevere through difficulty and suffering.

6. Fruitful Practices Relating to Communication Methods

- Use culturally appropriate Bible passages to communicate God's message.
- Communicate the gospel using the heart language, except in situations where it is not appropriate.
- Use a variety of approaches in sharing the gospel.
- Share the gospel using tools or methods that can be locally reproduced.
- Sow broadly.
- Use the Bible as a means of sharing the gospel.
- Share the gospel in ways that fit the learning preferences of their audience.
- Be aware of Islamic terms and thought patterns and use them as a bridge to sharing the biblical gospel.

7. Fruitful Practices Relating to Fruitful Teams

- Be united by a common vision.
- Build one another up in love.
- Have effective leadership.
- Employ the various gifts of their members to serve the task.
- Adapt their methods based on reflective evaluation and new information.
- Have at least one person with high language proficiency in the heart language.
- Engage in corporate prayer and fasting.
- Expect every team member to be involved in sharing the gospel.
- Value their female members as essential partners in ministry, facilitating their active involvement.

8. Fruitful Practices Relating to Characteristics of Fruitful Faith Communities

- Use the Bible as the central source for life, growth, and mission.
- Worship using indigenous forms of expression.
- Practice baptism.
- Value networking together.
- Be committed to one another as extended family, practicing the biblical "one another" commands.
- Redeem traditional festivals and ceremonies.
- Share meals and practice hospitality.
- Share the Lord's Supper in culturally appropriate ways.
- Seek to bless their wider community.
- Involve women in culturally appropriate forms of ministry.

For more information, see https://www.fruitfulpractice.org

DISCUSS

We are not asking you to decide if God is calling you to live in another country. The real question is one of lordship: "Is there anything God might ask of me that I would refuse to do?" If you answer yes, then missions is not the issue here – lordship is (Colossians 3:17). Once you and God have settled that matter, you can join the growing number of people on a global journey for God's glory.

Accomplishing God's plan for the world will require untold numbers of believers, with many different skill sets and callings, giving their talents to the Lord to be used for his purposes. Each of the roles below could be fulfilled in a variety of ways. Where could you begin?

GO: Serving God in a different culture

SEND: Send missionaries through encouragement, logistics, and finance

WELCOME: Care and befriend those who come for work, study, or a new life

MOBILIZE: Share the vision of God's mission with people you know

LEARN: Explore and study what God has stirred up in your heart for mission

PRAY: Commit to praying for a specific missionary, ministry, or people group

For more information, see https://www.omf.org/us/6-ways/

1. **Consider your passions and skills, as well as the circumstances of your life and location and abilities. Now answer the following questions.**

   a. What is your plan?

   b. What actions to move your plan forward have you determined to take?

   c. Stop and pray right now for God's enablement.

   d. Who will you share your plan with for accountability?

2. **Now prioritize the ideas you have, deciding which steps should be first. Are there other steps you need to add?**

3. **Regardless of the steps you have chosen, you cannot accomplish them without God's empowerment. A busy life, other commitments, Satan's attack – so many things may stand in the way of enacting your plan.**

   a. What obstacles do you face?

b. Describe the attitude and approach you believe God wants you to adopt in response to these obstacles.

MEDITATE

1. **Read Psalms 86:9 and 98:2-3, and Philippians 2:9-11. Meditate on your part in God's plan for every people, tribe, language, and nation. Record what occurs to you as a result of your reflections.**

2. **Memorize Psalm 46:10: "He says, 'Be still, and know that I am God; I will be exalted among the nations, I will be exalted in the earth.'"**

Our prayer is this: that the greatest passion of your life is to know Jesus Christ and to manifest his glory; moreover, that your daily walk with Jesus Christ will connect with his global purpose of calling Muslims to worship and glorify the God of all nations.

INTERCEDE

OVERVIEW OF THE MUSLIM DIASPORA IN EUROPE AND NORTH AMERICA

Many of Europe's great cities — Moscow, Paris, London, Madrid, Rome, Berlin, etc. — have become home to a multitude of cultures and languages as immigrants and refugees have flooded the continent. Some seek opportunity and education. Many refugees still arrive fleeing war, famine, economic hardship, and other circumstances.

As of January 2020, there were 23 million non-EU citizens living in the European Union.[55] In 2020, 471,000 applied for asylum in the EU, down from a high of 1.3 million in 2015.[56] Among these newcomers are many Muslims. In Europe, Islam continues to grow through a high birthrate as well as immigration: Islam is now Europe's second largest religion.

Many native Europeans view the newcomers as outsiders, and they are often disproportionately blamed for urban problems. Columnist Thomas Friedman charges that Europe has not been successful in "integrating and employing its growing Muslim minorities, many of whom have a deep feeling of alienation." Almost 26 million Muslims comprise 4.9 percent of Western Europe's population in 2016.[57]

A young Algerian Muslim man living in Brussels expressed the tension many immigrants feel: "I don't belong anywhere. We go to North Africa on holiday and are laughed at because of our poor Arabic. Then we come back home to Europe where we're the 'dirty Arabs.'"

The Muslim population of North America has also grown dramatically since the 1960s. Although the U.S. Census Bureau does not collect data on religious background, a 2018 Pew report indicates that the United States is home to 3.5 million Muslims.[58] Canada has just over a million Muslims and could double by the 2030s. There are now over 2,100 mosques in the U.S.[59]

In the United States, many Muslims are from North Africa and the Middle East (14 percent) or South Asia (20 percent) descent.[60] Not all these immigrants are Muslims. A significant number of Arab-Americans are Christians, and many South Asian immigrants are Hindus and Sikhs. America is also home to about 500,000 Iranians.[61] Twenty percent of Muslims in the U.S. are black.[62] Forty-two percent are U.S.-born citizens, half of which are at least third generation Americans.[63] Of the one million international students who came to the United States in 2015, over 100,000 came from Muslim majority countries.[64]

Not all of North America's Muslims are recent immigrants. Approximately 21 percent of Muslims are converts to Islam.[65] According to research done by the Pew Foundation, 67 percent of U.S. converts to Islam are African-American; 35 percent are from Caucasian and other racial backgrounds.[66] However, other studies have shown that many converts to Islam do not remain in Islam long-term.

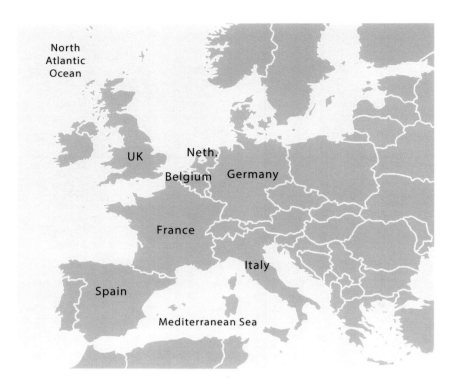

Approximate Muslim Population[67]

France	5.7 million	8.8%
Germany	4.8 million	5.7%
United Kingdom	4.1 million	6.3%
United States	3.5 million	1.1%
Italy	3 million	4.8%
Spain	1.2 million	2.6%
Canada	1.1 million	3.2%
Belgium	1 million	7.6%
Netherlands	1 million	5.1%

PRAYER POINTS:

- Pray that European and North American churches would reach out in love to Muslim immigrants.

- Pray that Muslim refugees would find freedom through Jesus Christ and be welcomed by Jesus' followers wherever they are resettled.

- Pray that Muslim-background believers would boldly share their hope in Christ with Muslim immigrants.

"Give me the love that leads the way, The faith that nothing can dismay, The hope no disappointments tire, The passion that will burn like fire; Let me not sink to be a clod: Make me Thy fuel, Flame of God."
– Amy Carmichael (1867–1951)

GLOSSARY OF MUSLIM TERMS

Abu Bakr (ah-boo **bah**-kuhr) – first male convert, Muhammad's sponsor; first Caliph

Aisha (ah-**ee**-shah) – Muhammad's "favorite" wife (third), daughter of Abu Bakr

Ali (ah-**lee**) – Muhammad's cousin, fourth Caliph (Sunni), successor (Shi'a), married to Fatima

Allah (**ahl**-lah) – God (Arabic)

Allahu Akbar (ah-**lah**-hoo **ahk**-bahr) – "God is the Most Great" (Arabic)

amulet – charm, talisman

Anatolia – geographic designation of Asia Minor

animism – belief that creation is alive with spirits; worship of spirits

Arabia – Southwestern Asian peninsula

Arabic – Semitic language; language of Qur'an

Arabs – native speakers of Arabic

Aya (**a**-yuh) – verse of a Sura in the Qur'an

Bedouin – nomadic desert Arabs

Believers – monotheists; believers in God

Bismillah (bihs-mihl-**luh**) – "In the name of God;" invocation of God

Cairo – capital of Egypt; Islamic center

Caliph (khah-lihf) – God's representative; former political-spiritual Islamic ruler

Christendom – Christianity as geographical entity

Creed – witness; Shahada, first Pillar

Crusades – Christian campaigns to reconquer Holy Land, Jerusalem (1100s–1300s)

Diaspora - the movement, migration, or scattering of a people away from their homeland

Eid al-Adha, Id al-Adha (eed uhl-**ahd**-huh) – Feast of Sacrifice, end of Hajj

Eid al-Fitr, Id al-Fitr (eed uhl-**fooh**-tihr) – Feast of Breaking the Fast, end of Ramadan

ethne (ehth-**nay**) – the nations, people groups (Greek)

evil eye – envious glance bringing evil

al-Fatihah (ahl-**fah**-tee-huh) – opening Sura (Qur'an), repeated in salat

Fatima (**fah**-tee-muh) – Muhammad's and Khadija's daughter

fellahin (fehl-lah-**heen**) – member of laboring class in Arab country who lives off land

folk Islam – popular Islam

Gabriel – archangel God sent to reveal Qur'an to Muhammad

gospel – Jesus' message; Injil

hadith, Hadith (hah-**deeth**) – traditions; collection of literature which interprets Islam; sayings of the Prophet

Hagar – Ishmael's mother

hajj (**hahj**) – pilgrimage (to Mecca); fifth Pillar

halal (hah-**lahl**) – permitted, lawful

haram (hah-**rahm**) – forbidden, unlawful

Hijra (**hihj**-ruh) – Muslim emigration (Mecca to Yathrib [Medina]) in AD 622; the Islamic lunar calendar commences from this year, when Islam was launched as a state and movement.

Holy Black Stone – sacred stone in wall of Ka'aba

Holy City, The – Mecca, Saudi Arabia

Holy House – Ka'aba (**kah**-ah-buh)

Husayn, Husain, Hussein (hoo-**sayn**) – Ali's son, Muhammad's grandson; mourned by Shi'a

Ibrahim – Abraham, father of Ishmael and Isaac

imam (ee-**mam**) – spiritual leader, professional cleric

infidel – non-believer, polytheist, idol worshiper

Injil (ihn-**jeel**) – original, uncorrupted Gospel; present-day New Testament

Isa al-Masih (**ee**-sah ahl mah-**seeh**) – Jesus the Messiah (Arabic)

Ishmael – father of Arabs, Ibrahim's eldest son

Islam (**ihs**-lahm) – submission; monotheistic Muslim faith

Jehovah Jireh – name for God; the God who provides, Al-Razzaq in Arabic

jihad (**jee**-hahd) – struggle; internal for holiness, external to extend umma; popular media term for holy war

jinn (**jihn**) – species of spirits, both evil and helpful

Ka'aba (**kah**-ah-buh) – Holy House in Mecca, holds Holy Black Stone, center of Islam

kafir (**kah**-fihr) – ungrateful, unbeliever, infidel

Kalimat Allah (kah-lee-**maht ahl**-lah) – The "Word of God," Isa

Khadija (khah-**dih**-jah) – Muhammad's first wife

Mahdi (**mah**-dee) – the rightly guided one; the coming Imam, a Messiah-like world leader who will return in Shi'a Islam

masjid (**mahs**-jihd) – mosque (Arabic)

MBB – Muslim-background believer: others prefer BMB, believer from a Muslim background

Mecca – Islam's holiest city in Saudi Arabia; place of the Ka'aba, Muhammad's birthplace

Medina (mah-**dee**-nuh) – Islam's second holiest city; in Saudi Arabia

Messenger of God, The – Muhammad

Middle East – Southwest Asia

minaret – tower of mosque for call to prayer

mosque (**mahsq**) – Muslim house of worship, prayer

Muhammad (moo-**hahm**-mahd) – last Prophet and founder of Islam (570–632)

mullah (**mu**-luh) – Muslim religious leader or cleric

Muslim (**moos**-lihm) – one who submits; follower of Islam

Ottoman – Turkish Empire (1300–1922)

Paradise – reward after death; heaven

People of the Book – Jews and Christians (Qur'an)

Persia – remnants of ancient empire in Southwest Asia

Pillars of Faith – the five religious duties of Muslims

popular Islam – common Muslim practices, addressing problems of fear, powers, and spiritual beings

prophet – a warner, divinely inspired

Prophet, The – Muhammad, God's Messenger

Qur'an (Koran) (kohr-**ahn**) – sacred Scriptures of Islam (in Arabic)

Quraysh (koor-ray-**ihsh**) – dominant Arab Meccan tribe (Muhammad's)

Ramadan (rah-mah-**dahn**) – sacred month of the fast

rasul (rah-**sool**) – apostle; messenger; a prophet; title of Muhammad

salaam (sah-**lahm**) – peace; a greeting of peace

salat (sahl-**laht**) – five required, daily ritual prayer times; second Pillar

saum (**suh**-woom) – the fasting, third Pillar, especially during Ramadan

Shahada (shuh-**ha**-duh) – Creed, witness; first Pillar

Shari'a, Shari'ah (shuh-**ree**-uh) – ideal Islamic law; God's will expressed in the Qur'an, the Hadith, and the Sunna

Shi'a (plur., **Shi'i**) (**shee**-uh, **shee**-ee) – minority branch of Islam (10 percent); followers of Ali

shirk (**shuhrk**) – association of partners with God (as in the Trinity); considered polytheism

Sufi, Sufism (**soo**-fee) – Islamic mysticism; seeking awareness of God's presence, relationship to him

Sunna (**soon**-nuh) – established, normative precedent; based on Muhammad's example, from Hadith

Sunni (soon-**nee**) – largest branch of Islam (87 percent); derived from Sunna

Sura, Surah (soo-**ruh**) – chapter of Qur'an

tawhid (**tahw**-heed) – term used to express the unity of God, the only God

Traditions – Hadith

umma, ummah (**oom**-muh) – Muslim community; the unified, equal people of Islam

Wahhabi (plur., **Wahabiyin**) (wah-**hah**-bee, wah-**hah**-bee-yeen) – conservative branch of Sunni Islam

worldview – system of values; one's view of reality

Yathrib (**yehth**-rihb) – destination of emigration (hijra); renamed Medina

zakat (zah-**kaht**) – statutory alms tax (for needy); fourth Pillar

DEMOGRAPHICS OF THE VISION 5:9 NETWORK

NUMBER OF ORGANIZATIONS

2003: 7
2004: 14
2005: 17
2006: 17
2007: 17
2008: 25
2009: 50
2010: 75
2011: 112
2012: 126
2013: 163
2014: 177
2015: 180

NUMBER OF WORKERS SERVING AMONG MUSLIMS

2004	6,787
2009	7,710
2011	9,159
2013	13,000

COMPOSITION OF WORKERS

ORIGIN

Global North serving cross-culturally — 66%

Global South serving near-culturally — 15%

Global South serving cross-culturally — 19%

GENDER

FEMALE 52% 48% MALE

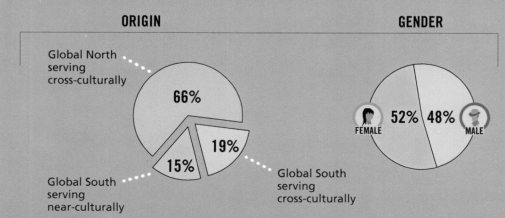

177 TOTAL MEMBER ORGANIZATIONS

59 International Sending Organizations

32 Networks and Partnerships

8 Foundations/ Resourcing Entities

17 Denominational Entities

30 National Sending Organizations

31 Mobilization and Training Organizations

WORKER ACTIVITY PROFILES

JUDICIOUS INTERCESSORS
Prayerful, culturally sensitive — **12%**

TRADE-LANGUAGE STRATEGISTS
Broad impact and reproducible methods — **18%**

WORD-CENTERED ADVOCATES
Committed to sharing scripture — **44%**

ORALITY OVERCOMERS
Local languages and oral strategies — **26%**

FRUITFUL THEMES IN WORKER PRACTICES

- Fluency
- Reputation
- Social Networks
- Varied Scripture Use
- Storying
- Intentional Multiplication
- Prayer
- Courageous Witness

VISION 5:9
— REVELATION —

ENCOUNTERING THE WORLD OF ISLAM

After studying *God's Heart for Muslims*, join us for *Encountering the World of Islam.*

Encountering the World of Islam (EWI) guides you on a journey into the lives of Muslims around the world and in your neighborhood. Through this comprehensive course, you will learn about Muhammad and the history of Muslims. Gain insight into today's conflicts and dispel western fears and myths. Discover the frustrations and desires of Muslims and learn how to pray for and befriend them. EWI provides a positive, balanced, and biblical perspective on God's heart for Muslims and equips you to reach out to them in Christ's love.

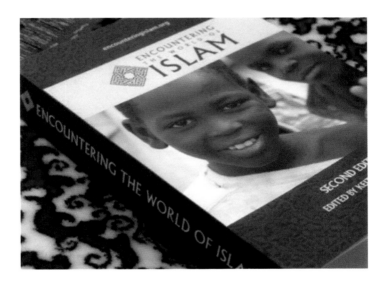

What is the EWI course?

EWI is a twelve-lesson course that combines typical learning assignments with experiential activities and online interactions for an integrated multi-disciplinary learning environment. Each lesson is taught by a different Muslim or Christian expert. This course is engaging and life-changing as a result of the rich combination of methods of instruction. The textbook itself has more than eighty authors providing a broad range of perspectives on Muslims.

Participants say:

"I am learning that I have to ask God to help me see through His eyes and not mine. He knows how to reach hearts and he will show me if I wait for him to show me. I believe God has always and will always help us if we are willing to be humble enough."

"I so appreciate how people-focused this course is, specifically in that our interactions with Muslims should be about listening, understanding, and getting to know the whole person not just their religion. We are called to love our neighbors as ourselves."

"My attitude towards Muslims has changed, even though I did not know it needed to change; my ability to make relationships with Muslims has improved, even though I did not know it needed to improve; and I have been encouraged in how God will use me."

To learn more about *Encountering the World of Islam*, to find a course location near you, to enroll in an online class, or to order the *Encountering the World of Islam* textbook, go to https://www.encounteringislam.org.

RESOURCES

FREE STUDIES AND RESOURCES

- *Xplore*, mobilization.org/xplore - Help Christians embrace their God-given role to make His name famous throughout all the earth.

- *Go Mobilize*, mobilization.org/go-mobilize - Learn to start a mission movement among friends, church, and family.

- Common Misconceptions about Muslims - encounteringislam.org/misconceptions

- Questions Muslims Ask - encounteringislam.org/muslimquestions

- Missions Catalyst - a weekly e-magazine, missionscatalyst.net

FREE PRAYER RESOURCES

- 1010prayerandfasting.com, 10/10 Initiative - For Gospel Engagement: A Prayer Guide of the Vision 5:9 Network

- Encounteringislam.org/prayercards

- Pray30days.org - culture, background, and prayer requests for Muslim peoples.

- Prayercast.com - beautiful short videos narrated by believers from each country and background prayed for.

- Globalprayerdigest.org - a daily prayer guide for unreached people groups.

- Operationworld.org - facts and prayer requests on every country of the world.

BOOKS ON MUSLIMS

- *From Seed to Fruit: Global Trends, Fruitful Practices, and Emerging Issues Among Muslims*, J. Dudley Woodberry, ed. missionbooks.org

- *Fruit to Harvest: Witness of God's Great Work among Muslims*, Gene Daniels, Pam Arlund, Jim Haney, eds. missionbooks.org

- *Where There Was No Church: Postcards from Followers of Jesus in the Muslim World*, EJ Martin missionbooks.org

- *Where There is Now a Church: Dispatches from Christians Workers in the Muslims World*, James Nelson, ed. missionbooks.org

- *Encountering the World of Islam*, Keith Swartley, ed. encounteringislam.org

- *Fruit to Harvest: Witness of God's Great Work among Muslims*, Gene Daniels, Pam Arlund, Jim Haney, eds. missionbooks.org

WEBSITES

- Peoplegroups.org - Muslim people group profiles

- Fruitfulpractice.org - Vision 5:9 Fruitful Practices Research website

- Mobilization.org - Center for Mission Mobilization website

- Globalmobilization.org - Global Mobilization Network website

ENDNOTES

1 https://www.gordonconwell.edu/center-for-global-christianity/

2 peoplegroups.org/

3 peoplegroups.org/

4 https://countrymeters.info

5 https://countrymeters.info

6 https://www.worlddata.info/languages/arabic.php

7 https://worldpopulationreview.com/country-rankings/muslim-population-by-country

8 https://worldpopulationreview.com/country-rankings/muslim-population-by-country

9 https://worldpopulationreview.com/country-rankings/muslim-population-by-country

10 https://worldpopulationreview.com/country-rankings/muslim-population-by-country

11 https://www.pewresearch.org/fact-tank/2017/01/31/worlds-muslim-population-more-widespread-than-you-might-think/

12 https://www.pewresearch.org/fact-tank/2017/01/31/worlds-muslim-population-more-widespread-than-you-might-think/

13 https://www.pewresearch.org/fact-tank/2018/01/03/new-estimates-show-u-s-muslim-population-continues-to-grow/

14 https://www.gordonconwell.edu/center-for-global-christianity/resources/status-of-global-christianity/

15 https://www.pewforum.org/2011/01/27/future-of-the-global-muslim-population-sunni-and-shia/

16 https://www.peoplegroups.org/

17 https://www.grd.imb.org/research-data/

18 https://www.peoplegroups.org/

19 https://www.peoplegroups.org/

20 https://www.peoplegroups.org/

21 Jason Mandryk, Operation World, 7th Edition (Downers Grove, IL: InterVarsity Press, 2010), p. 22.

22 https://www.worldatlas.com/articles/arabic-speaking-countries.html

23 https://worldpopulationreview.com/country-rankings/muslim-population-by-country

24 https://countrymeters.info/en/World#religion

25 https://www.peoplegroups.org/Explore/AffinityBlocDetails.aspx?rop1=A001

26 https://worldpopulationreview.com/country-rankings/muslim-population-by-country

27 https://worldpopulationreview.com/country-rankings/muslim-population-by-country

28 https://www.peoplegroups.org/Explore/AffinityBlocDetails.aspx?rop1=A012

29 https://www.peoplegroups.org/Explore/ClusterDetails.aspx?rop2=C0318

30 https://www.grd.imb.org/research-data/

31 https://www.grd.imb.org/research-data/

32 https://www.peoplegroups.org/Explore/AffinityBlocDetails.aspx?rop1=A015

33 https://www.grd.imb.org/research-data/

34 https://www.grd.imb.org/research-data/

35 https://www.macrotrends.net/cities/20053/baku/population

36 https://www.peoplegroups.org/Explore/AffinityBlocDetails.aspx?rop1=A008

37 https://www.peoplegroups.org/Explore/AffinityBlocDetails.aspx?rop1=A008

38 https://worldpopulationreview.com/country-rankings/muslim-population-by-country

39 https://www.peoplegroups.org/Explore/PeopleDetails.aspx?rop3=100036

40 http://grd.imb.org/research-data/

41 https://www.peoplegroups.org/Explore/AffinityBlocDetails.aspx?rop1=A005

42 https://www.grd.imb.org/research-data/

43 https://www.peoplegroups.org/Explore/AffinityBlocDetails.aspx?rop1=A005

44 https://www.peoplegroups.org/Explore/ClusterDetails.aspx?rop2=C0114

45 https://www.grd.imb.org/research-data/ Sum of both Horn of Africa and Sub-Saharan African blocs.

46 https://worldpopulationreview.com/country-rankings/muslim-population-by-country

47 https://www.pewresearch.org/fact-tank/2017/01/31/worlds-muslim-population-more-widespread-than-you-might-think/

48 https://www.peoplegroups.org/Explore/AffinityBlocDetails.aspx?rop1=A013

49 https://www.peoplegroups.org/Explore/AffinityBlocDetails.aspx?rop1=A004

50 https://www.grd.imb.org/research-data/

51 https://worldpopulationreview.com/country-rankings/muslim-population-by-country

52 https://worldpopulationreview.com/country-rankings/muslim-population-by-country

53 https://www.peoplegroups.org/explore/ClusterDetails.aspx?rop2=C0077

54 https://www.peoplegroups.org/explore/ClusterDetails.aspx?rop2=C0077

55 https://www.ec.europa.eu/eurostat/statistics-explained/index.php/Migration_and_migrant_population_statistics

56 https://www.ec.europa.eu/eurostat/statistics-explained/index.php/Asylum_statistics

57 https://www.pewforum.org/2017/11/29/europes-growing-muslim-population/

58 https://www.pewresearch.org/fact-tank/2018/01/03/new-estimates-show-u-s-muslim-population-continues-to-grow

59 Leila Fadel, "Being Muslim in America," National Geographic, May 2018, p. 58.

60 Leila Fadel, "Being Muslim in America," National Geographic, May 2018, p. 58.

61 "Iranian-Americans and the 2010 Census: Did We Shrink?". Retrieved 4 July 2014.

62 Leila Fadel, "Being Muslim in America," National Geographic, May 2018, p. 58.

63 Leila Fadel, "Being Muslim in America," National Geographic, May 2018, p. 58.

64 https://www.inside.collegefactual.com/blog/how-many-international-students-are-in-the-us

65 Leila Fadel, "Being Muslim in America," National Geographic, May 2018, p. 58.

66 https://www.pewforum.org/2017/07/26/religious-beliefs-and-practices/

67 https://worldpopulationreview.com/country-rankings/muslim-population-by-country

VISION 5:9
—— REVELATION ——

We are a network of people committed to seeing church planting movements among every Muslim people group.

Learn the best practices that workers are discovering in planting churches in Muslim communities.

Join us and thousands of believers around the world in praying for breakthroughs in every Muslim people group.

www.1010prayerandfasting.com

To learn more, visit www.vision59.org

WHAT IF GOD'S INVITING YOU INTO

A GLOBAL STORY?

XPLORE

DISCOVER
GOD'S WORD, GOD'S WORLD, AND GOD'S WORK

Xplore is a powerful small group study designed to help you and your church play a significant role in God's global story.

Learn more at **mobilization.org/Xplore**

Xplore is a resource of the Center for Mission Mobilization. mobilization.org